THE LAME GOD

May Swenson
Poetry Award Series
Volume 16

THE LAME GOD

poems
by

M. B. McLatchey

UTAH STATE UNIVERSITY PRESS
Logan

© 2013 M. B. McLatchey
Foreword © 2013 Edward Field

Published by Utah State University Press
An imprint of University Press of Colorado
5589 Arapahoe Avenue, Suite 206C
Boulder, Colorado 80303

 The University Press of Colorado is a proud member of
the Association of American University Presses.

The University Press of Colorado is a cooperative publishing enterprise supported, in part,
by Adams State University, Colorado State University, Fort Lewis College, Metropolitan
State University of Denver, Regis University, University of Colorado, University of
Northern Colorado, Utah State University, and Western State Colorado University.

Publication credits appear on page 66, which constitutes an extension of this
copyright page.

Cover art "Hephaestus II" by Scott Eaton. Used by permission.
Cover series design by Barbara Yale-Read

ISBN 9780874219074 (cloth)
ISBN 9780874219081 (paper)
ISBN 9780874219098 (ebook)

Library of Congress Cataloging-in-Publication Data

McLatchey, M. B.
    The Lame God : poems / by M. B. McLatchey.
        pages cm. — (May Swenson Poetry Award Series ; Volume 16)
    ISBN 978-0-87421-907-4 (hardback) — ISBN 978-0-87421-908-1 (paper) — ISBN
978-0-87421-909-8 (ebook)
    I. Title.
    PS3613.C574L36 2013
    811'.6—dc23
                                    2013030755.

For John

Ille colit terras, illi mea carmina curae
—Virgil

CONTENTS

Let me warn the reader: it takes courage to read this book. This heart-breaking sequence of poems on the abduction of a daughter hit me like a ton of bricks, and I had to put it aside several times. But what courage it took to write it. Though there are many poems on grief, and even on crime—websites are devoted to them—I have never come across a book of poetry like this before.

I hesitate to mention a popular genre like "true crime" in relation to the high art of poetry, but *The Lame God*, like that genre, speaks with such power because its subject matter is so unspeakable. While M. B. McLatchey's lyricism here seems indifferent to narrative and this collection recoils from the piecemeal reportage of the crime novel, each poem in the sequence draws us closer to the scene of the crime. What we are not told only enlarges the horror—*and the pathos*. Its controlled language and emotional restraint remind me of my acting teacher, who used to say: "Actor weeps, audience sleeps. Actor with-holds tears, audience weeps." This book proves it.

Striking about the style is its dead seriousness. The tragedy explored here has grounded the author in such a profound, such a justified, seriousness that there is no room for anything else—no playfulness, no witticism—no relief, except in the cathartic release of poetry. In fact, it seems a heroic act—an act of survival—that she has sculpted these poems so austerely, and so appropriately, like a Classical urn. I was surprised to find Classical references in poetry again, after they had disappeared for the past half-century, but they work. For in the violence of the ancient Greek myths, McLatchey finds an appropriate landscape of metaphor.

May Swenson, in her poem "Snow in New York," spoke of the power and magic of words. Dealing with my own sorrows and ter-rors, I have always felt poetry to be a healing art, and it has helped me through my worst times. Indeed, the Inuit taught that the right words actually make things happen (in spite of W. H. Auden's dictum that they don't). Like a survivor of other horrors, one can never be recon-ciled to such a monstrous event as this book reveals. Nor does reli-gion help much. Yet, in exploring such a grief through the language of poetry, McLatchey *makes things happen*—she gives a voice to those too grief-stricken to speak, and she refuses to allow us to suffer in silence.

It is a hard fact that, to the artist, everything is material. We grit our teeth and use even the most personal catastrophes—our own and those of others—to make art. This is what the Classical authors did, and this is what M. B. McLatchey has done with her great subject in this book. The effect is powerful, and ultimately, *The Lame God* proves that if our traumatic experiences don't destroy us, they can produce masterful works, in which human nature rises to its heights.

Edward Field

In his preface to the *Lyrical Ballads*, Wordsworth insists that the poet's subject need not come from personal experience, but it must *become* personal experience. In committing to a regimen of repeated witness in the world, the poet's very *impulses* and *habits of mind* are transformed until, over time, the poet's work becomes the poet's life. When parents lose a child to an abduction and murder and then descend into a well of grief, the poet writes as a way to call to them until it becomes clear that she must descend into the well herself— to know the water level there, the damp walls, the underbelly of this abomination.

The poems in this collection are "well poems"—conceived and drafted in a pit of loss and rage, with its shadowy promise of redemption. The story that this book tells is true. No names have been changed to protect the innocent—the innocent have already seen the face of evil, smelled its breath, learned its customs.

This book is offered in memory of Molly Bish and in homage to her mother, Maggie Bish, who encouraged me to "keep talking about this; keep writing." It is also for Adam Walsh, Amber Hagerman, Levi Frady, Maile Gilbert, and Morgan Chauntel Nick. It is for the roughly 2,000 Mollys and Adams and Ambers and Levis and Morgans that are reported missing daily to the National Center for Missing and Exploited Children; it is for Deb Cucanich and for the tireless caseworkers at the Department of Children and Families. This book is for three girls held captive and abused for a decade in a house in an American city—but it is especially for the child who has not yet pried open a bolted door, borrowed a neighbor's phone, and announced to a 911 operator, "I've been kidnapped and I've been missing . . . and I'm here."

M. B. McLatchey

I used to wonder, Amaryllis, why
You cried to heaven so sadly, and for whom
You left the apples hanging on the trees;

'Twas Tityrus was away. Why, Tityrus,
The very pines, the very water-springs,
The very vineyards, cried aloud for you.
                                    —Virgil, *Eclogue I*

Acting quickly is critical. Seventy-four percent of abducted children
who are ultimately murdered are dead within three hours of the
abduction.
                    —Federal Bureau of Investigation and
                        National Crime Information Center

The weight of the receiver in my hand:
the down bird in my palm first lifting you.
The counselor's words: rehearsed, a burlesque bland.

The shift in time, the shift to looking through
her lens: today you are just one of two
hundred lost. My eyes fix on our bright fence.

I say your name, but you are no one new —
caught in an ancient book that she'll condense.
I want her to discuss you in the present tense.

I want the gods to stop pretending love
calls the departed home. We called you
with our various loves, had hope, hovered

over still fields; made wind like the gods do
before they come unhinged, let their rage loose
on an unresponsive yield. Fields gone deaf

and dumb; unshaken, fruitless ground, unmoved
by a neighborhood of mothers who left
their own to find you — tables, like mine, set.

I want the gods to swallow their prayers
whole. Choke up my child like the Olympians —
a girl, unbruised by her journey down their

throats. I want her at my table: fruit, alms
that the gods, I see, can give or take — balm
for the irritations I caused, or they

caused; gifts between us or perhaps among
themselves — a girl that they'll barter away.
I'm here. And I'm willing to talk, or trade.

THE RESCUE

It's not about closure. It's about justice.
　　　　　　　　　　　　—John Walsh, father to Adam Walsh

Today in the news: *Miraculous Rescue.*
　　　An uncle drags a shark to shore

to save his near-dead nephew.
　　　A bull of a shark, the arm that it tore

from the boy when he waved for help
　　　fueled the beast's palate; its tail

in the uncle's grip, a blur of blood claret and kelp;
　　　the husks from his palms, a grim and edible kale.

I want a shark that I can wrestle
　　　and make it spit you out. To make it yearn

for its strength, to thrash about as I nestle
　　　its nose in my grip. I want to turn

you loose from a palpable place: a well, a shed, a jaw.
　　　I want the monster to face me and beg for the law.

Nothing. Nothing at all. And distant cries,
apparently, are not the things we hear
but call out in our sleep —
a sudden fear or reckoning
that sits us up in bed, waking,
slowly waking, and then the shaking,
and then the sober lying down again.
It's what your father does:
a ritual cry as if to call you home
or as if to say goodbye —
goodbye — goodbye. Tender reunions,
or a gradual dying. The pacing round
your room, his mourning dance.
His search for answers — or grace.
How could no one have heard
you call our names?

And then the invocation
from his knees, the terrible refrain
that always shakes him:
the simple word *please*
a passerby reported hearing —
but did not stop. Entreaty?
Or your supplication
to a deaf God? Your effort
to appease? Or perhaps it wasn't
words, but the shivering of limbs
shedding their leaves.
Can nature sympathize?
or only echo how we call,
tremble, breathe? *Please*,
the blades of grass, rows of hedges,
swaying trees must have uttered
to a universe of passers-by.

Please, to a pantheon of gods,
also bowed, also recasted,

as if to mirror your appeal —
or worse, perhaps
as if to see past it.

AMBER ALERT

A white Ford, black gate, Georgia plate,
squeezes into our lane. In the back, a Whitetail

tagged and slashed from her chest to hind legs
looks back at us. Her eyes a dark glass.

Opening day for deer hunting. Cars pass
and pass. In a field, lightning bugs darted

and flashed in your hand. Half-girl, half-doe,
you started and stopped, palms cupped.

Someone carried you off and we cheered
for the boy in the clay, his heel on home plate.

It was a beautiful steal.
Did he thank the deer for her head

when he knelt above her? When he opened
her middle to empty inedible parts? When,

for a clean job, he severed her windpipe and —
hunter's nectar — he saved her heart?

Alone without me and from home afar
Ah! May the frost not hurt thee, may the sharp
And jagged ice not wound thy tender feet!

—Virgil, *Eclogue X*

MANDATUM

Lifting you onto our kitchen counter top,
I almost stumbled. You were four, a fish hook
caught in your foot. Salt from your tears on my cheek:
          Mommy will fix it.

Footprints the police find in the yard. A trail!
Map perhaps! Or a fossil, a sacrifice —
tendril of fledgling vines that shone through her skin —
          beating, translucent.

Feigned expertise, but I talked you through it: Look
what a beautiful, golden-haired fish someone
caught! And you hung on the hook as I curled you free
          neither one breathing.

Beating, translucent. Not the picture I gave.
Police want a weight, height, age. So difficult
not to measure her in steps, first syllables —
          beacons like lodestars.

Not a drop of blood in the sink when we washed
up, as if the hook had cauterized the wound —
Hobbling away, you gave me our sign, thumbs up:
          I was a big girl.

Small for her age, according to the line drawn
on our kitchen wall. A penciled life stage — line
tentative and conscious, covenant maker
          poised to retrace her.

For the minutes, hours, days
that once, with a girlish
yearning, I wanted back.
For the slap in the car when you were two.
For — trusting your safe return —
not missing you.
For trusting the gods.
For my second-rate
circumspection;
for trusting the odds.
For the tremor
of heat in the small
of your hand in mine — a fear
of strangers,
of shadows,
the dark.
My little bank swallow,
I called you.
For this city
of sand banks
and sound-proof walls.
For teaching you to love
the same: the thief
and the devout.
For teaching you not to shout.
For us still uncovering
your terror — layer by layer.
For this sputtering sound of real prayer.

Watering. Rainwater is better than tap.
More in the summer when the weather is
warm. Another concern: the size of the pot.
Small pots need frequent watering.

You tipped back your head,
mouth open as if to drink.
Rain on your cheeks, lips, chin.
Tonic from heaven, you said.

Proper light. This will yield
grass-green leaves, and not the burnished
hue of too much exposure — and not
the flaccid spine of a dark, cold space.

Leaves, rank and rotten that you pressed
in your hand, held under my nose.
I mimed a squeezed throat;
play acted death's stranglehold.

Orchids need air. In their natural
habitat, they often grow anchored
in a tree with little or no soil
in a cool, shaded place.

Breathe, breathe in your new habitat —
a tree? a loft? a well? a grave?
Breathe like a stem that — if I have to —
I will dry and press and save.

Here again. The way you used to
wake us — rouse us with that impatient stare.
A stubborn, fair-haired, fifth-grader,

you make the same requests. I say them
with you. Isn't this what happens
when one of us brings water to the dead?

The private shift to living only sometimes
with the living. Eight months among the missing
and you come padding back in your white socks

and jeans; specter of grief we locked away
before it made us more dry-mouthed and speechless
than our counterparts in dreams. Grief like light

encounters in a half-sleep: your moist face
in a morning mirror. And how, each night
you casually resume, at every threshold

to every listing room, that awkward lean —
the one you would do when you could not ask,
but knew that we could help.

Your bony shoulder
barely touching the wall;
your right foot crossing the other.

So young and old. So much the pose
of one who is neither coming nor going.
It's difficult to know why we should wake.

Still, every day we rise like guardians
ex officio, like gate-keepers
to a city of passing shades — each one

a new acquaintance with your face.
Each one a new petition for deliverance
of the innocent and quaking.

MUSEUM

Historical pieces, these things of yours:
a deflating ball; a bike not on its kick, but propped

against a garage wall; a crestfallen lacrosse stick. Tours
have come through as if walking the way of the cross:

neighbors with pasta, a friend to awkwardly drop off
a borrowed skirt. Police with their pens and pads

making calculations. A press release for the missing, accosted,
kidnapped, or dead. Your photo, a ghost of a soul you had.

Musée des Beaux Arts for the ambushed, the dispossessed,
for guardians like us, who did not guard their watch,

conservators of hellish thoughts — thoughts too wretched
for talk. Prayers in place of a fight we would have fought

had you called out. But what, after all, can our prayers do
except repeat prayers from the past and that surely God knew?

Hush little baby,
no more fears. Momma's gonna
make you a bed of prayers.

In a knoll of bedclothes, another battle
unfolds. Soldiers in green against tan.
In his hand, a toy bird, round and plush,
twice the size of the plastic men,
waits for his command.

And if these weary prayers
aren't heard, momma's gonna
get us a homing bird.

Cher Ami. He introduces him
to me. Message carrier through gunfire
in his grandfather's tale. A myth meant to
teach him what nature makes right.
All he has in his arsenal tonight.

She'll carry your note and your sack of coins
to the man who took your sister —
and we'll be rejoined.

We tallied our treasure; we mortgaged
the house. How much is a sister
worth?

Before you wake, before you blink:
Sister, you, and pigeon
like our fingers linked.

Some china from England, a grandmother's
pearls. How much for a ten-year old girl?

And if that homing bird
won't fly, momma's gonna
make us a road nearby.

Her image in the news like a missing
clue. A girl in black and white,
whom he looked up to

when sisters came in colors —
last seen in powder blue.

These tears like crumbs we'll leave
from you; sighs, tower bells
we'll sound out too.

And he — like smelling salt —
could make his sister come to
just thinking her name from across the room.

And if those crumbs and bells don't —
I know, baby.
I know. Shhh.

An accident with prisms
but in Greek it means
Beautiful form to see.
So renewed was its maker
to look through a tunnel
of mirrors and find,
not his face,
but a tumbling symmetry.
Hundreds of sheets
of cathedral glass
shattering like shards
of earthenware.
Swatches from
a cardinal's robe
folding and unfolding.
Rivers of molten gold.
A sky that implodes.
Multiple minds
and a heart in flames.
What we go to
but cannot construe.
It is with
his new hope
that I wrap it
and give it to you.

ON RECOGNIZING SAINTS

As if to find new icons for her life
or as if — piece by piece — to dismantle mine
she scans our purchases too consciously.
Flips through a magazine I'm embarrassed
to be buying. Studies its regimen
for shapely thighs; asks me — because she's heard —

if drinking wine is good for nursing.
The shift from idle chit-chat to appeal.
Camille, her name tag says. Camille
of olive skin and violet nails
with long metallic tips, who flashes
her lover's sucking marks

like her stigmata. Camille who isn't
showing yet — but like Crivelli's virgin
martyr, Catherine, peers sidelong at me
and leans decoratively against her register
as Catherine did against her studded wheel.
So clearly Catherine that I want

to look away — or kneel.
And yet, Crivelli would have
framed her differently: a martyr
tucked away with other martyrs
in a predella of muted colors, quiet
suffering. None of this heart-to-heart —

this girlfriend talk that brings to mind
a string of small petitions
and makes me say my part.

I range O'er rocks, through echoing groves. . . .
As if my madness could find healing thus,
Or that god soften at a mortal's grief!

—Virgil, *Eclogue X*

MORNING OFFERING

Dear god and all the saints,
stay near,
especially today
or I shall betray you —
not like Judas
or Marcus Brutus,
not like Jason's Medea,
who draped his
lifeless toddlers
across her cheating husband's knees —
but like the mother
of a child, who sees
how lines are crossed
and newly-painted fences
scaled or thwarted.
Please, god,
watch over
those
who smile
and ask me how
I am holding up.
I am holding up
just long enough
to find the trespasser
in his own world
and — god have mercy —
his defenseless
little girl.

Always a condition, some passionless pledge.
Eurydice's sweet ascent dependent on
her lover's forward march,

his heart stone-dead, head bent.
One glimpse her way, as lovers
or as watchful guardians

naturally do and nature comes undone:
she spirals, grotesque figurant,
into a dark, dank pit, worlds from

a healing sun. Or Aeneas, goddess-born,
destiny's champion, barred from his father
in Elysium — until his warrior's fist unwound

to pluck a jeweled limb. Who set these terms?
Not Orpheus in his upper world, who only
yearned for something he never surrendered

to be returned. A girl whom he had —
with music, art, good talk and open palms —
loved and attended. A bough made of gold

for a glimpse of one's kin — a father,
a wife — and you, hardly half-grown,
too good to have noticed the chasm you had

been charioted through. Too small, too —
Instead of living, we review. You were
not goddess born, nor forest nymph.

We were not heroes who knew
how to barter with gods; how to
tunnel our way to their subterranean

lair; how to make enough noise
that you'd hear us conspiring above;
how to keep you propped up

and aware of your splendor. None of it
like we remembered. The stars watched
unconcerned. You did not leave

a basket of stems upturned. No guardian pointed
us southward to advance our reasoning; birds
did not mark their homes in a renewal of seasons.

Instead, a bank officer for our loan; a detective,
heartbroken he says, *because he has a girl of his own.*
His tender clichés: *no stone unturned, no stone.*

Perhaps it was there in the tale all along.
What kind of ransom, after all,
does one bring to a pillager

who wants golden charms for his captive-queen
and already has his lamb to slaughter?
What other ending, but nature

denuded, petrified, desperate for water
when a nine-year-old stops listening for a sign,
a breeze to climb, someone calling *daughter?*

In the parish hall of Saint Anthony's Catholic Church,
pictures of murdered children in our hands,
we huddle in a sphere of folding chairs
and a flickering fluorescent light. Some lean
near the coffee and coffee cake that, each week,
has the same floury smell of sympathy
and each week, the same sour taste.

By the tissues, a painted soapstone statuette —
our patron saint. O, the watches and keys
and gloves that appeared at your feet! A ruse
that my mother relied on to make me believe
that our smallest petitions are heard,
that events, with the proper appeals, can be reversed,
that almost anything lost can be retrieved.

As a girl I chanted your name while I followed the trail:
pockets, under the bed, under the sofa cushions,
pockets again. *Something's lost and can't be found.*
Please, St. Anthony, look around. When it didn't turn up,
I brought you coiled vines, like the petals I bring
to my daughter's room as if to stir up stale air,
or as if to confirm I was still yours and you
were mine — and the search would resume.

Look at the priestess of talismans I have become:
her saint card from First Communion in my purse;
lodestones for paperweights at work; for good luck,
a horseshoe-shaped necklace under my shirt:
the crescent shape of the sacred moon-goddess
in Peru or the bow of the Blessed Mother's cradling arm,
arch like the threshold of her sacred vulva,
twine like the helix of lovers.

Look at the virtuoso that was finally birthed,
who would use this ring of linked hands
not for fellowship or grace, not *to make*
my peace on earth, not to lay my gifts

at your feet and give up the search,
but to summon the face she petitioned
and conjure a curse.

A god needs worshippers. I starved them
to make the god blink — and he did. I'll tell
you what justice is: it's a mother's revenge,
enough to give the gods a taste of her hell;

enough to make them come crawling for a deal —
give us our congregation; we'll give you your girl.
Each time the seasons cycle, I steel
myself — each winter that first without her.

Eternal winter. As for her father on earth
who, after his stroke, shuffles some mornings
to his daughter's door. *Where is she?* he turns
to ask me, and I hold him, his tired and worn

face, tell him the story again: *drills like devotions, then this cold bed.*
And I nod as he rocks in my arms and wants someone's head.

SNOW GLOBE

La Tour Eiffel. An April-snow
like pollen covers
a patch of stolid tulips.

From the first platform, he leans
over slick railings,
leans as if in Keats's scheme

to drop and drop a red corsage
to a woman below.
I see it now: this is the one

of 300 steel workers, who tumbled
to his death clowning around.
Her promise is to keep him

from his fall by gazing back —
his sentinel, his figurine
against the filmy wash of elements

against the fading colors in a dome.
I shake it — not for snow —
but to marvel at their hold.

We have lived to see what never yet we feared.

—Virgil, *Eclogue IX*

THE RAPE OF CHRYSSIPUS

She came home bone by bone. First her shin bone, then her skull.
In the end, 26 of Molly's bones came home to us.
                                    —*Mother of 16-year old, Molly Bish*

For the rape of Chryssipus, King Laius suffered.
        The gods saw what he took —
                a young boy's chance

to play in the Nemean Games, to make his offerings
        to Zeus, to win his wreath
                of wild celery leaves, advance

the Greek way: piety, honor, and strength. He raided
        their heaven, not just a small boy's frame.
                Their justice

was what Laius came to dread: a son that would take
        his mother to bed,
                a champion of the gods, an *Oedipus*.

We called on the same gods on your behalf, asked
        for their twisted best:
                disease like a Chimera to eat

your Laius piece by piece; a Harpie, who might wrap
        her tongue around his neck
                and play his game of breathing

and not-breathing that he made you play.
        Medusa's curse in stone — and a Golden Ram
                to put you back together bone by bone.

At the beach, in the shallows wading, oddly alone.
In the mirror of my dressing room, the curtain thrown
while you enter and leave the stage. *Encore!* I call and you

reappear for a bow. Or, our quiet-voice game at the market,
you called *Bury-Me,* where you hid under house things in the cart:
bier of bath towels, shower-curtain for a shawl.

At a traffic light, to my right, that quirky smile —
a Vanilla Wafer in your hand. We study each other for a while.
Your face moist and tanned, your yellow bangs combed and straight.

Or the way you balance your tea between your palms — afraid of spills —
in a diner booth that swallows your small frame. It's not the pills.
I quit them when, even with wine, they wouldn't take.

I see 20/20 through the ache. I see you before they brought
you home in parts. Echoes reflecting a mouth, thumb, heart,
in your first term you slept suspended — a test, or a dare

to the ones who submerged you again once you came up for air.
I see you — before they delivered you bloated and blanched —
in a string of days, scheduled and planned.

A bath I draw.
Water, like open flora,
that buoys me — legs, belly,
arms brushing a porcelain
river's edge — my hair,
a grassy sedge.

A film we rent — popcorn as usual.
Out of the blue, but of course,
it is part of the script, a girl
in a minor role, eight or nine
exits with a flourish:
Later alligator — your line.

In bed, the room dark,
your father's moist face
against mine.

Our dutiful attendance
at gatherings — a cook out,
with games for the adults.
A reunion in a gymnasium.
After mass, a baby
baptism.

Another tonic and gin.

The shadows of the dead
had to drink from it
to forget their previous lives.

I wish this for you
from time to time:
that seconds into
his twisted vaudeville act
something flickered —
the prow of a boat perhaps,
and in precisely the moment
his props were unpacked —
wire, packing tape, ballast

to steady your limbs
as you sank —
you felt the boatman's ladle
at your lips and drank.

BINGO NIGHT FOR MISSING AND EXPLOITED CHILDREN

Before we went underground. Before you fell through a gyre with no sound.

If one piece were unwound. If you had run. If we had looked for you sooner. If you had screamed. If the gods had intervened.

Nascent. Still blooming, the orchid on your window sill. A thrill of color.

Gone. Gone. Gone. Gone. Gone. Phantom limb. If the soul leaves the body, we did not feel it go. Nothing and everything cloistered in stone.

Omens we left for others. Ripples on a resting pond. The whistling of a breeze. The imprint on the ovaries.

A GLASS OF ABSINTHE
after Degas

At first we pass them, unstudied
as a snapshot where marginal subjects

have slipped in. A disenchanted pair
off-center and off-level, lean

like bags of flour into the singular
pitch of a café's genial keel; no ballast here

except for the pool of milky licorice —
a teetering glass of absinthe.

So startling to see how everything was made
to dovetail; how the zigzag of empty tables

between us and the luckless couple traces
a brooding loneliness, a composition

so boldly calculated that we can hardly face
its draughtsmanship. Powdered pigments

molded into figures whose back sides blaze
like butterflies caught in an ashen rain

in mirrors propped behind them.
The proprietor had thought the glass might

brighten the place. But, there is no changing
history or the reflections of our lives.

CATHARSIS

A portly man on TV says he's eating jelly donuts
since his doctor recommended more fruit. My head
tucked beneath your chin, I feel you grin. A welcome joke —
what Aristotle called *catharsis*: the comedy channel in bed.

A piecemeal purging meant to clear our minds, a chance
to graft, like patchwork, the wreckage of our lives
onto a campy figure, cheer for him; love him for dancing
when the gods single him out, pile on their twisted trials.

As if — for a few moments — we are watching someone else's
life unfold. Pizza and beer, you my armchair, tucked in our sheets.
As if — for a few moments — we have climbed up from some well
to lounge on sun-baked stone, take in the Dionysian Mysteries:

lore of the vine — seasons, grapes, wine. Nothing ever truly dying.
And us, tender initiates, laughing so hard we're crying.

See, sick at heart I drive my she-goats on.

—Virgil, *Eclogue I*

THE BOY'S LAMENT

A history lesson tossed
beside his bed: a warrior's speech
in a boy's sullen script.

A teacher's note
about which nothing is said.
I pick things up,

but leave some of the mess
as if to show him how
to do the same.

For Virgil's little herder
nature's laws were just as plain:
missing shepherd, fallow grain.

1

Two small hands, like two voices apart
glide parallel across familiar keys.
To you it feels like sowing rows of peas.
The sheet of music, an old planting chart

that — somehow — you already know by heart.
The swift, smooth stream of action: a kinetic melody.
And, if you are disturbed, we know it means
a kind of riot: repeating and repeating from the start.

Whatever is in range, you touch
perhaps a hundred times: your coda,
or a hundred brusque hellos. As for the rest of us:
a level grove. Never too much
from one hand without the same part owed
by the other. A synchrony of planting and pulling up.

2

How did we miss it? Your ocean-blue eyes
blinking like a pair of flashing lights. Your call
but so alarming that we could not tolerate
the thought of flashing back a weak reply —

except, of course, to say there was no need for tying
shoelaces twice; no need for always following
the left foot with a cautious right; no need for swallowing
and shrugging like a hunchback climbing

out of someone else's skin; no need to tap your glass
with both forefingers producing that short salvo of clicks.
Rituals that repeat your presence in our lives, little fits
that we must be attentive to, that we must pass
through. Necessities, not wants, delivered and enshrined in tics
that make us doubt the obvious: a simple smile, songs in a singing
class.

3

In Medieval France, a neurologist, Georges Gilles de la Tourette
had tried to drown the ticking monster with a tonic.
Instead, the monster drank and drank with a demonic
thirst. Gilles was the first to feel regret

for wanting the monster dead, or at least quiet.
But, why should he — or anyone — have heard symphonic
sounds in his patients' grunting, their chronic
sniffing of the world's boundaries? They must have met

him at his worst: his calling spasms mischief;
angry at God, but eager to do God's work
of exorcising devils from a boy who could not sit
still. We chastised the same boy before it
dawned on us that there was nothing lurking,
only the steady tapping for attention, or for mercy.

4

A quick-fire volley of five pats
delivered to the heads of each: a brother
and an unaffected cat. Lover
of music, but neither instrument reacts.

They've gone to sleep; they know your waxing
and your waning, your hovering
between day and night. They know the other
side to this conductor. Your endless tasks:

tonight, arranging an elaborate army corps
to guard the porcelain bank of a bath, checking
and rechecking them at their ports.
A sergeant by a mammoth whitewashed door
shifting at every count of four, tentatively inspecting
a passage for your tour.

5

At times, we want to know the ticking
heroes, to see Samuel Johnson lumber
through London's Enlightenment; to know his number
game: five steps — then hold — to make it six

on crossing any threshold. A man of letters bound
to God, and subject to his senses. Like walking in a slumber
he weaved his way around walls, unencumbered
to find — heart in his mouth — higher ground.

Higher ground. It's what we wish for you.
And not the pyre of England's ticking witches. And not
the lonely tiles of plastic soldiers who withdrew.
Or, take this level ground you brought us to: tornado in a bottle.
You love the constant stream of oily blue spiraling through
clear water. Shake it again. Feel the circular pull of love renewed.

MYTHOLOGY

In this early light, the veins of a leaf —
the leaf that you were before you fell

into a lake — pulse beneath
your cheek. I lean over your crib

the way another mother must have
looked into a strange forest pool

to follow the wake of something
swimming past. Asleep, you are delivered

from her watch into mine. I see her
finger circling the water's edge.

Mid-celebration, a voice asks us to stand —
mothers for whom he says, *Let's give them a hand.*
Neighbors, their children, husbands look up

adoringly and clap. *The hand that rocks*
the cradle. . . . Most laugh. Some even finish
his adage — a kind of *Amen.* I sit in my pew;

my reflexes wooden, dull, missing his cue.
Your cradle, still in the attic; still so much to do.
After mass, a gathering in the function hall.

Doughnuts and coffee with powdered cream,
mothers with powdered cheeks.
Wallets spring open and photos of children

fall out; children who have married, had their own,
gotten jobs, divorced, moved back home.
No one asks. A parish registry of births

and deaths is all our news: your name there
two times in cursive like some Delphian refrain;
two baptisms — one blessed, one cursed

and a trail gone cold. In the end, a blessing,
awkward lingering. *It was good to have*
the chance to talk and mix.

I went home, mixed a tonic and gin,
said a prayer for your murderer's mother and —
for your sake and hers — practiced standing again.

Instead of the soft violet, instead of the gleaming narcissus, the thistle rises up and the sharp-spiked thorn. Strew the turf with leaves, shepherds, and build a tomb.

—Virgil, *Eclogue V*

Spring and its bright clichés.
The seasonal resolve
with which our neighbors
take to the earth. Rakes
like divining rods.
The search for bulbs
as if to stir a life
or as if to turn up nerves
too well adjusted
to an underworld.

Look how they change
their tools: from rake to hoe
to spade
to little brush
to coax or lure
their small heads out.
So earnest in their work
it's difficult to know
whom to love.
You in your roots —
recumbent, lush —
or these,
who seem to need me
more above?

SONG OF DAPHNIS

White babies-breath
glued
to a cinnamon heart.

Pink and blue ribbons
looped
through a tiny hook.

Bows
like emerging chrysalis
Did you make this?

I bend, imagining
his doughy hands
tying the delicate knot.

Mirror, mirror, let her go. Daughter, you are not home,
but trapped in a cool, glass pool. Portals like this
will sap us: thresholds, I'm told, when an ending
like yours occurs. No curtain fall. No denouement.

How restless these unfinished themes made you.
In school, a moved rock at Easter
in a pop-up book. A lesson in leaving us firmly
behind. No need for looking back. No need to ask —
though you did — *Where did he go?* Comical,
had you not been so earnest, turning the pages.
Even then, you wanted answers, some kind
of fair play: a knock-out blow, a judgment day.

In 4th grade, that essay, *Finish the Story Another Way*
you honed and re-honed. *My new ending changes everything*,
you complained. And of course, that was your teacher's plan:
to force your hand; to make you concede that all was as it should be;
that endings — in life, as in art — are like Gordian knots
meant to be sliced with a single sword-stroke by a man
already hand-picked by an oracle and the gods.
Too hard an assignment then and now.

The summer before you disappeared:
when you swam out too far, a floating dock
that I pointed to. Your medley of strokes to prove
you could get there alone: freestyle, frog kick,
butterfly. *Stand by*, you seemed to say
but no need for us to swim out. When you reached
the dock, your clownish wave — a signalman
performing a flag semaphore: *all safe on board*.

We hung on the shore and waved back *hello*
or *goodbye* like I am waving faintly now. Your
silhouette rocked with the planks — wood, water and you
had commingled somehow. Darling, this time swim
out to that dock — or another — for us, for sure.
But more than ever, for your own sake.

Even then, I suppose we knew it was some kind of drill.
Even then, we knew it was more than a game.

The game was not to look but feel
the slow drag, the rise

and fall, the quiet revolt of crests
gaining an underworld; to know in our heels

the moment of their advance: languid, insidious.
"Sanriku!" one of us would call —

a notice to the rest that it was imminent
And with one lift, a solidarity,

we'd throw ourselves beachward,
tossing and rolling in a curled force.

Submerged, I would hear that call
like water's moan, or like the heaving sobs

of Asian fishermen, who felt too late
the slip of plates, the buckling floor,

the little missionary wave passing
beneath their boats; who, steeped

in so much grief, never knew
the clarity that follows every quake —

when there, for just an instant,
the contours of the seafloor

are mirrored in the water
around our waists.

They see how lightly tragedies begin: old friends
approach, trade jokes, then ask the whereabouts
of someone else. Inconsequential chit chat.
I know by training what to think: invoking absent ones;

that's nature out of balance. But I stay quiet
and watch my best take turns reading aloud.
Premonitions, prayers, misgivings
all uttered much as we ourselves utter such things

without implying real belief in astral influence
or providence. In the mutilated versions
that Restoration audiences knew
finding the art in grief was just the same:

the principal requirement of loss.
Then, all the afterthoughts of obvious
but distant analogues. This morning's work
is metrics — harmless stuff, except for one:

a girl whose lovely throat warbles
what ought to be our longest vowels —
our sad approach. I make her try again,
knowing she'll have to do the rest herself.

A high point in her act:
Rings of blue smoke swirl

above her head like kisses
floating off a palm, or like balloons

of varnished silk that stretch
and lift her toward a parting draft.

A mix of comic strip and something raw
that worked in Lichtenstein's pastiche

of lines and polka dots; yet, somehow,
coming from her lips these figures

make us shift and sip — and sip again.
What is it makes us look away

as if remembering things to do at home?
Is it the clear distinction: what she sings

and what she knows? That unexpected
nimbus of true thought?

Easier, no doubt, to look through
little comic blocks, dream-like

and Byzantine — present,
yet one remove from present scenes.

There's a snake lurking in the grass.

—Virgil, *Eclogue III*

As a girl, I learned to hurl a curse
so it would hurt. The skill, not in the words
but in the work: bringing the self to feel

another's losses as though they were
one's own. And then, like an informer
against the heart, delivering the blows.

It frightened me to see a hex take hold
in a friend's eye, to see the crushing
sorrows one can summon with the mind.

Tonight, in the ashen shadows of your room
those curses seem to linger like stray dogs
reminding me, as our small petitions do,

of our double lives; our tendency
to come to terms too late. Your breadth,
like oatmeal's bloom, circles them in a breeze.

Above us, light that should comfort: glow
-in-the-dark stars careen like clockwork
through a black sky. For a lamp: a shuttle that turns

unceasingly over a dimly-lit earth.
I cover you again, although this August night
is still and though it's me that's shaking.

With a different girl behind us, this stillness
might be our grace. Instead it keeps me here
tonight not praying really, but pacing.

With an ease that belies his theme
my boy slumps into a mold of his own small back.
Chair or taffrail? The waves blend with his thoughts.
And far, far out of range, I search my heart for a send off:

To follow a runaway's lead? His optimism?
To see our little horrors and be social with them?
A summer breeze. And now the pages turn themselves;
he shifts and shifts. Perhaps the helmsman stares

now at the flaming try-works, sees the shapes: harpooners
poling, pitching that hissing mass — a reckoning
so stark he slips into a soporific dream
then suddenly comes to, but dead astern, his mind ignited

wondering how to save the ship from being brought to lee.
I read that scene until I could recite it. But now,
he lays the book like open wings across his lap
and basks and basks in summer's luxurious light.

I watch him like a swabber come to save a listing ship
and keep a kind of vigil while he naps.
Was God above young Ishmael as he packed his bag
for Cape Horn, the Pacific? Or, in New Bedford,

when he read the fate of whale men? An average,
good-hearted, dreamer at the masthead.
Watcher not watching, chatting with Queequeg.
O little dreamer, never in more danger

than on your sunny perch. Move your foot or hand
an inch, loosen your grip — and midday,
in the fairest weather, with one half-throttled shriek,
you drop through the transparent air into the summer sea.

Always in the distance,
burnt brown combines sweeping up
spools of wheat. My sons sleep
in the back seat — the younger one
bowed over; the other up straight
like a sun-drenched sheaf.

Up ahead, one sheer pool after another
that the heat lays down. *Day stars*
(the older one calls them) spring up
from the pools and usher us on,
then flicker and steam.
A Dakota we've never seen.

The steady re-inscribing of a field of rows;
the shearing of their braided tips
in order to bring something good
to wheat and goldenrod. A simple plan
like a coat of colors meant to unravel
thread by thread — and threshing it,

figures so small I can hardly interpret them.
Are they brothers? Father and son?
Brothers, since elders give up the wheel
more easily than this. And look how
the bigger one stands, then suddenly
disappears like the grain he's reeling in.

I reach back to wake the older one:
solicitude, or a favoritism
that I had thought might pass.
Or a reckoning of our lives
that comes when the light slants
like this, as if we are looking through

more than window glass. I pat
his leg to comfort, or to bless him,
or to brush some divination off.
But he is already looking out — and oddly —

seems to know what I can't bear to ask
myself or this Dakota God.

Consider what each soil will bear and what each refuses.

—Virgil, *Eclogue VII*

LEAVING THE MAINLAND
En route to Key West

The last resort as some wags dub it. And now
for the first time since leaving the mainland
we feel it. So narrow an approach, the road we're on
seems less a slip of land than a channel of water.

And everywhere the doubling back of life scenes:
bitterns teetering on one leg as if to remain
prescient of two worlds — this one that warms us
through car glass, and the other a stirring life

submerged. Island of bones. So overwhelmed
were they by life's remains — so many bones —
that de Leon and trails of others found there.
The terrible name must have given breadth

to their worst fears. Ships like theirs
brought to grief by poorly marked reefs
or the lure of a light on a cow's tail.
And after disaster, the call — but not for help —

among the islanders. *A wreck!*
Prosperity from ruined ships — a life
no one had entertained. Still, there they were
chasing submerged treasures. A slip in judgment

perhaps. But given the choice between limestone
too hard for digging graves or an ocean
of pyramids, who could blame them —
certainly neither of us — for wanting to live?

Red paint on an upturned wooden mouth.
Speech found for what was not spoken.

Old wood, a speaking through
timber and hollowed throats.

But the puppeteer,
the one with the breath

imitates so well — almost humanly —
what the breathless one would sound like

if she could speak. A bonded frame that —
like your first days in my arms — goes limp,

deaf and dumb, eyes closed,
without the ventriloquist's hold.

Inanimate limbs — once blossoming
on a fertile trunk, fed by a spring —

now culled and rearranged
to look like the living thing.

SONGS OF THE IMMORTALS

"We won't quit until we figure this out"
—Maj. Ray Tuttoilmondo, Galveston County Sheriff's Office

Prayers for Dead Girl Found on Beach.
This was the banner they gave you.
Found in a box and washed ashore,
Baby Grace, they named you. For a day,
for one sun-bleached day, you bathed
and dried in a summer light and open
air. Strangers, like sirens, inched near
as if they remembered you — someone or
something they'd seen before. Sirens
with ancient petitions, deafening songs
that the gods might wring out your lungs,
might right this wrong; that the Nereids
might sew up your skull,
might comb your sea hair;
that the fisherman
who plucked you from his net
might remember your eyes as pearls —
a shimmering blue —
and not as the closed, hard shells
that hid us from you. *Grace,*
as in beauty or clemency?
In the likeness they sketched
they drew you smiling, a toddler
glad to be sent down a river of snook
and clay. Glad for the drift-wood
cross above your feet. Glad
for a canticle of gulls
fighting, fanning each other
for scraps of a crab: hull . . . meat.
Glad, it would seem, for the shells
in place of flowers —
an almost hallowed ground.
Glad for an end to appeals,
rest for the hound.

Remember when your father went?
Your mother packed his things and sent them
off —

to Goodwill,
to the Salvation Army.

One day of stuffing boxes, labeling them
then it was done.

As if they had been
straightening out closets for years.

Or in case it happened as it did — napping
on a sofa in April. Perfect month.
A perfect month for going, she said.

Now when we're all so mindful
of a life ahead.

How could she stay behind
like that? Call it a perfect event?

It must have started earlier for her:
the body's long lament.

THE ARRANGEMENT

1

Because we were getting old enough
our instructor took us to look at (not to touch)
some pictures grown men drew.

We tripped like new recruits through orderly rooms.
Some were sternly directed to carry their shoes
as we made our hushed advance. In the dim hall

we could hear a classmate whimpering
as she would whenever she felt too far from home.
Her tears a kind of prelude to the work itself:

Flowers in a Vase — more paint than flowers
whose stems arched away, whose poppies
bleated and sprayed yellow tears

on our starched uniforms, on the perfect walls.
All the way home, the yellow hung on our clothes.
The bus took us sluggishly along, and we felt the road

under its beefy wheels change to a luminous river of paint
and the trees gave up their souls in Autumn's clay glow.

2

I knew what it meant but not really.
So I took the stairs two by two for you, like any other day.
In my pocket, paintings on postcards, a stick of gum.

In the kitchen below, Dad had grown small beside the cakes
the ladies brought. He would not eat, he would not speak
to relatives in the hall, and the relatives awkwardly leaning

on end tables like faded photos of themselves.
Mother was proud to find me at my prayers
and honoring the adults who were clearly "spent."

When she pressed her head to mine, I felt her hair
like fingers on my brow: a gesture she'd learned
from you, mother to mother, and was teaching me now.

And, this was "hard" and "each of us will have his own lament."
It took all I had to steady my temple to hers —
to keep my sorrow apart — as we planned

the next few hours: where the aunts would sleep
and who would order the flowers.

AUBADE

We wake in scenes that tell us
what we dreamed. Like Pilon's

warm gisants, my head turned
toward yours as if to close a space.

Your pulse oddly restored
in a sculptor's bloc. Nude

and appointed to reflect a light,
to make a chapel out of earth's

casualties. And then, inevitable
as the breath we have to take, the choice

we're granted in this early hour —
the brackish call of migratory waterfowl

or art's stony appeal: sealed
in a hall as statues of our decay

doomed, yet attached
in a docket of holy days.

1

He walked on thin legs, as Homer put it.
Hephaestus, born with a shriveled foot
that so humiliated Hera, she threw her son

into the sea. Once tossed from high Olympus,
he turned his frailty into grit: counter insurgency.
A *terra firma,* as opposed to the water she dreamed of.

His exile made him face his kind, build her a catbird seat —
a throne with a trick release. In the end, he hobbled,
motherless castaway, into their pantheon.

What was it made the Greeks admit him into their
heavenly suite? In their myths, his wit and craftsmanship.
But there was plenty of that to go around. A twisted foot

telegraphed a twisted mind — but not if he carried out
heroic deeds. Too hard — any mother could see —
a balancing act. Still, the symmetry! The playful scale

of damned and apple of their eyes. Twins on a coin,
a champion form: what men could learn to love;
what mothers wished was never born.

2

On this city bus, gods sit in rows: some absently
stare ahead, some drop their heads to doze. One
moves his lips as his hand passes over black beads;

one scans a tabloid for discounts, celebrities.
I am looking for him: the mug shot, the lineup's near-
match, the newspaper likeness, the witness's sketch.

The rope in his pocket they said he unwound
from your neck, the man with the radical limp
and the crown on his head. We are in the kingdom

of counter insurgency. Since you came home smaller
and cold, we have settled in among these forms: *horrors*
that are apparently not horrors, but the foreground to a god-

power untapped. *Mercy*, a tide that expelled you
like foreign matter. *Faith*, a dog that followed your
fading scent. *Forgiveness*, a mother boarding a bus,

her body buoyed by the crush of other bodies.
Do not worry, daughter. We are not leaving our watch
or showing our cards — just changing the guard.

What if we let you sing first? What if we look
for you with Mallarme's blank stare:
birds round an empty dish, stony limbs?

To tell the history of our grief
we settle for an empty doorway
and a maple leaf

or a woman with neck curls, named Jane,
changed by her poetry teacher's love
to a wren wound in light.

Elegies so resolute in wood
or wings that we forget the truer
measurements of unfinished things:

the distance between two disappearing
habits; the echo of a promise
lodged in a warbler's throat;

the length of a dreamy girl swinging
from her favorite limb; the ragged patch
below — our ground for spotting her.

If grieving is a way of working wood,
building thresholds, wrapping birds —
then hands will keep us tending things

too near. What if this June air
should circle, not fall on, our copper chimes
with the passiveness of prayer?

What if the breeze that would carry
a bird's perfect sorrow were to kneel
at the base of an oak, and refuse to rise?

ACKNOWLEDGMENTS

Heartfelt gratitude is due to the editors of the journals in which these poems appeared, sometimes in slightly different form:

The Adirondack Review for "Bingo Night for Missing and Exploited Children," winner of the 2013 *46er Prize*

American Poetry Journal for "Leaving the Mainland" and for "1-800-THE-LOST," winner of the *American Poet Prize*

The Anthology of New England Writers for "A Glass of Absinthe"

Beauty/Truth: A Journal of Ekphrastic Poetry for "Girl at Piano" and "The Arrangement"

Cider Press Review for "Snow Globe"

The Comstock Review for "Museum," "The Rescue," and "The Retrieval"

The DMQ Review for "Aubade"

Georgetown Review for "Oaths, Curses, Blessings"

The National Poetry Review for "Against Elegies" and "On Recognizing Saints," winner of the Annie Finch Prize

new south: Georgia State University's Journal of Art and Literature for "Amber Alert," winner of the *new south* Poetry Award

River Styx for "At the Grieving Parents Meeting"

Smartish Pace for "Catharsis"

The Southern Poetry Review for "Teaching the Tragedies"

The Spoon River Poetry Review for "Melville's Reader," "The Lame God," and "The Rape of Chrysippus," winner of the Editor's Prize

Willow Springs for "Sanriku," winner of the Vachel Lindsay Award

For their roles in developing this book's cover art, gratitude is extended to Scott Eaton (www.scott-eaton.com) for permission to use his digital sculpture "Hephaestus II" and to Ben Johnson (www.benjohnsonart.com) for his vision and contribution to the cover design.

ABOUT THE AUTHOR

M. B. McLatchey's work has appeared in *American Poetry Journal,* *National Poetry Review, River Styx, Spoon River Poetry Review, Georgetown Review, Ekphrasis, Beauty/Truth, Comstock Review, Emerson Review,* and many other literary journals. Her literary awards include the *American Poetry Journal's* American Poet Prize for 2011, the *Spoon River Poetry Review* Editor's Prize, the Annie Finch Prize for Poetry, the Vachel Lindsay Poetry Award, and the Penelope Niven Creative Nonfiction Award, and she has been a finalist for the May Swenson Poetry Award, the Rita Dove Poetry Award, the Lynda Hull Memorial Poetry Prize, the Lumina Prize of Sarah Lawrence College, the Robert Penn Warren Award, the William Faulkner Poetry Prize, the Richard Snyder Memorial Poetry Prize, the Muriel Craft Bailey Memorial Award, and the Erskine J. Poetry Prize.

Her academic awards include the Harvard University Danforth Prize for Excellence in Teaching, the Radcliffe Prize for Literary Scholarship, the Brown University Elmer Smith Award for Teaching, the Yeats International Summer School Graduate Fellowship, and Highest Honors from Williams College for her poetry collection *Advantages of Believing.*

She holds a master's degree in comparative literature from Harvard University, a master's in teaching from Brown University, an MFA from Goddard College, and a BA from Williams College. She has taught literature and writing at Harvard University, Rollins College, the University of Central Florida, and Valencia Community College. She is currently teaching writing and humanities at Embry-Riddle Aeronautical University in Daytona, Florida.

Visit her at: www.mbmclatchey.com

THE MAY SWENSON POETRY AWARD

The annual award in her name honors May Swenson as one of America's most provocative and vital writers. In John Hollander's words, she was "one of our few unquestionably major poets." During her long career, May was loved and praised by writers from virtually every major school of American poetry. She left a legacy of nearly fifty years of writing when she died in 1989. She is buried in Logan, Utah, her birthplace and hometown.